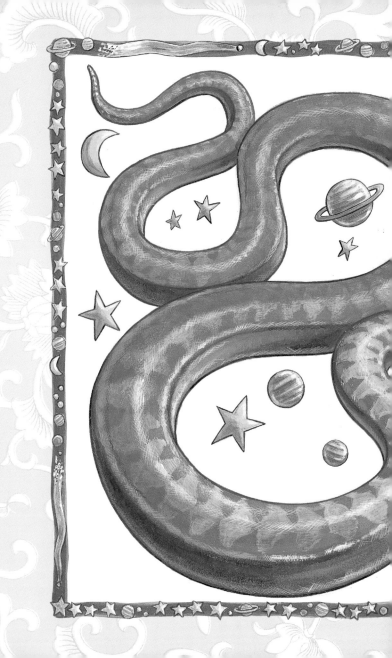

CHINESE
HOROSCOPES
FOR
LOVERS

The Snake

LORI REID

illustrated by

PAUL COLLICUTT

ELEMENT BOOKS

Shaftesbury, Dorset • Rockport, Massachusetts • Brisbane, Queensland

© Lori Reid 1996

First published in Great Britain in 1996 by

ELEMENT BOOKS LIMITED

Shaftesbury, Dorset SP7 8BP

Published in the USA in 1996 by

ELEMENT BOOKS, INC.

PO Box 830, Rockport, MA 01966

Published in Australia in 1996 by

ELEMENT BOOKS LIMITED

for JACARANDA WILEY LIMITED

33 Park Road, Milton, Brisbane 4064

The moral right of the author has been asserted.

Designed and created by

THE BRIDGEWATER BOOK COMPANY

Art directed by *Peter Bridgewater*

Designed by *Angela Neal*

Picture research by *Vanessa Fletcher*

Edited by *Gillian Delaforce*

Printed and bound in Great Britain by
BPC Paulton Books Ltd

British Library Cataloguing in Publication data available

Library of Congress Cataloging in Publication data available

ISBN 1-85230-766-8

Contents

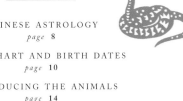

THE
SNAKE

8

*Why are
some people
lucky in
love and
others not?*

Chinese Astrology

SOME PEOPLE fall in love and, as the fairy tales go, live happily ever after. Others fall in love – again and again, make the same mistakes every time and never form a lasting relationship. Most of us come between these two extremes, and

some people form remarkably successful unions while others make spectacular disasters of their personal lives. Why are some people lucky in love while others have the odds stacked against them?

ANIMAL NAMES

According to the philosophy of the Far East, luck has very little to do with it. The answer, the philosophers say, lies with 'the Animal that hides in our hearts'. This Animal, of which there are 12, forms part of the complex art of Chinese Astrology. Each year of a 12-year cycle is attributed an Animal sign, whose characteristics are said to influence worldly events as well as the personality and fate of each living thing that comes under its dominion. The 12 Animals run in sequence, beginning with the Rat and followed by the Ox, Tiger, Rabbit, Dragon, Snake, Horse, Sheep, Monkey, Rooster, Dog and last, but not least, the Pig. Being born in the Year of the Ox, for example, is simply a way of describing what you're like, physically and psychologically. And this is quite different from someone who, for instance, is born in the Year of the Snake.

蛇

9

The 12 Animals of Chinese Astrology.

RELATIONSHIPS

These Animal names are merely the tip of the ice-berg, considering the complexity of the whole subject. Yet such are the richness and wisdom of Chinese Astrology that understanding the principles behind the year in which you were born will give you powerful insights into your own personality. The system is very specific about which Animals are compatible and which are antagonistic and this tells us whether our relationships will be successful. Marriages are made in heaven, so the saying goes. The heavens, according to Chinese beliefs, can point the way. The rest is up to us.

10

Year Chart and Birth Dates

UNLIKE THE WESTERN CALENDAR, which is based on the Sun, the Oriental year is based on the movement of the Moon, which means that New Year's Day does not fall on a fixed date. This Year Chart, taken from the Chinese Perpetual Calendar, lists the dates on which each year begins and ends together with its Animal ruler for the year. In addition, the Chinese believe that the tangible world is composed of 5 elements, each slightly adapting the characteristics of the Animal signs. These elemental influences are also given here. Finally, the aspect, that is, whether the year is characteristically Yin (-) or Yang (+), is also listed.

The Western calendar is based on the Sun; the Oriental on the Moon.

YIN AND YANG

Yin and Yang are the terms given to the dynamic complementary forces that keep the universe in balance and which are the central principles behind life. Yin is all that is considered negative, passive, feminine, night, the Moon, while Yang is considered positive, active, masculine, day, the Sun.

11

Year	From – To	Animal sign	Element	Aspect	
1900	31 Jan 1900 – 18 Feb 1901	Rat	Metal	+	Yang
1901	19 Feb 1901 – 7 Feb 1902	Ox	Metal	–	Yin
1902	8 Feb 1902 – 28 Jan 1903	Tiger	Water	+	Yang
1903	29 Jan 1903 – 15 Feb 1904	Rabbit	Water	–	Yin
1904	16 Feb 1904 – 3 Feb 1905	Dragon	Wood	+	Yang
1905	4 Feb 1905 – 24 Jan 1906	Snake	Wood	–	Yin
1906	25 Jan 1906 – 12 Feb 1907	Horse	Fire	+	Yang
1907	13 Feb 1907 – 1 Feb 1908	Sheep	Fire	–	Yin
1908	2 Feb 1908 – 21 Jan 1909	Monkey	Earth	+	Yang
1909	22 Jan 1909 – 9 Feb 1910	Rooster	Earth	–	Yin
1910	10 Feb 1910 – 29 Jan 1911	Dog	Metal	+	Yang
1911	30 Jan 1911 – 17 Feb 1912	Pig	Metal	–	Yin
1912	18 Feb 1912 – 5 Feb 1913	Rat	Water	+	Yang
1913	6 Feb 1913 – 25 Jan 1914	Ox	Water	–	Yin
1914	26 Jan 1914 – 13 Feb 1915	Tiger	Wood	+	Yang
1915	14 Feb 1915 – 2 Feb 1916	Rabbit	Wood	–	Yin
1916	3 Feb 1916 – 22 Jan 1917	Dragon	Fire	+	Yang
1917	23 Jan 1917 – 10 Feb 1918	Snake	Fire	–	Yin
1918	11 Feb 1918 – 31 Jan 1919	Horse	Earth	+	Yang
1919	1 Feb 1919 – 19 Feb 1920	Sheep	Earth	–	Yin
1920	20 Feb 1920 – 7 Feb 1921	Monkey	Metal	+	Yang
1921	8 Feb 1921 – 27 Jan 1922	Rooster	Metal	–	Yin
1922	28 Jan 1922 – 15 Feb 1923	Dog	Water	+	Yang
1923	16 Feb 1923 – 4 Feb 1924	Pig	Water	–	Yin
1924	5 Feb 1924 – 24 Jan 1925	Rat	Wood	+	Yang
1925	25 Jan 1925 – 12 Feb 1926	Ox	Wood	–	Yin
1926	13 Feb 1926 – 1 Feb 1927	Tiger	Fire	+	Yang
1927	2 Feb 1927 – 22 Jan 1928	Rabbit	Fire	–	Yin
1928	23 Jan 1928 – 9 Feb 1929	Dragon	Earth	+	Yang
1929	10 Feb 1929 – 29 Jan 1930	Snake	Earth	–	Yin
1930	30 Jan 1930 – 16 Feb 1931	Horse	Metal	+	Yang
1931	17 Feb 1931 – 5 Feb 1932	Sheep	Metal	–	Yin
1932	6 Feb 1932 – 25 Jan 1933	Monkey	Water	+	Yang
1933	26 Jan 1933 – 13 Feb 1934	Rooster	Water	–	Yin
1934	14 Feb 1934 – 3 Feb 1935	Dog	Wood	+	Yang
1935	4 Feb 1935 – 23 Jan 1936	Pig	Wood	–	Yin

蛇

12

Year	From – To		Animal sign	Element	Aspect	
1936	24 Jan 1936 – 10 Feb 1937		Rat	Fire	+	Yang
1937	11 Feb 1937 – 30 Jan 1938		Ox	Fire	–	Yin
1938	31 Jan 1938 – 18 Feb 1939		Tiger	Earth	+	Yang
1939	19 Feb 1939 – 7 Feb 1940		Rabbit	Earth	–	Yin
1940	8 Feb 1940 – 26 Jan 1941		Dragon	Metal	+	Yang
1941	27 Jan 1941 – 14 Feb 1942		Snake	Metal	–	Yin
1942	15 Feb 1942 – 4 Feb 1943		Horse	Water	+	Yang
1943	5 Feb 1943 – 24 Jan 1944		Sheep	Water	–	Yin
1944	25 Jan 1944 – 12 Feb 1945		Monkey	Wood	+	Yang
1945	13 Feb 1945 – 1 Feb 1946		Rooster	Wood	–	Yin
1946	2 Feb 1946 – 21 Jan 1947		Dog	Fire	+	Yang
1947	22 Jan 1947 – 9 Feb 1948		Pig	Fire	–	Yin
1948	10 Feb 1948 – 28 Jan 1949		Rat	Earth	+	Yang
1949	29 Jan 1949 – 16 Feb 1950		Ox	Earth	–	Yin
1950	17 Feb 1950 – 15 Feb 1951		Tiger	Metal	+	Yang
1951	6 Feb 1951 – 26 Jan 1952		Rabbit	Metal	–	Yin
1952	27 Jan 1952 – 13 Feb 1953		Dragon	Water	+	Yang
1953	14 Feb 1953 – 2 Feb 1954		Snake	Water	–	Yin
1954	3 Feb 1954 – 23 Jan 1955		Horse	Wood	+	Yang
1955	24 Jan 1955 – 11 Feb 1956		Sheep	Wood	–	Yin
1956	12 Feb 1956 – 30 Jan 1957		Monkey	Fire	+	Yang
1957	31 Jan 1957 – 17 Feb 1958		Rooster	Fire	–	Yin
1958	18 Feb 1958 – 7 Feb 1959		Dog	Earth	+	Yang
1959	8 Feb 1959 – 27 Jan 1960		Pig	Earth	–	Yin
1960	28 Jan 1960 – 14 Feb 1961		Rat	Metal	+	Yang
1961	15 Feb 1961 – 4 Feb 1962		Ox	Metal	–	Yin
1962	5 Feb 1962 – 24 Jan 1963		Tiger	Water	+	Yang
1963	25 Jan 1963 – 12 Feb 1964		Rabbit	Water	–	Yin
1964	13 Feb 1964 – 1 Feb 1965		Dragon	Wood	+	Yang
1965	2 Feb 1965 – 20 Jan 1966		Snake	Wood	–	Yin
1966	21 Jan 1966 – 8 Feb 1967		Horse	Fire	+	Yang
1967	9 Feb 1967 – 29 Jan 1968		Sheep	Fire	–	Yin
1968	30 Jan 1968 – 16 Feb 1969		Monkey	Earth	+	Yang
1969	17 Feb 1969 – 5 Feb 1970		Rooster	Earth	–	Yin
1970	6 Feb 1970 – 26 Jan 1971		Dog	Metal	+	Yang
1971	27 Jan 1971 – 15 Jan 1972		Pig	Metal	–	Yin

Year	From – To		Animal sign	Element	Aspect	
1972	16 Jan 1972 – 2 Feb 1973		Rat	Water	+	Yang
1973	3 Feb 1973 – 22 Jan 1974		Ox	Water	–	Yin
1974	23 Jan 1974 – 10 Feb 1975		Tiger	Wood	+	Yang
1975	11 Feb 1975 – 30 Jan 1976		Rabbit	Wood	–	Yin
1976	31 Jan 1976 – 17 Feb 1977		Dragon	Fire	+	Yang
1977	18 Feb 1977 – 6 Feb 1978		Snake	Fire	–	Yin
1978	7 Feb 1978 – 27 Jan 1979		Horse	Earth	+	Yang
1979	28 Jan 1979 – 15 Feb 1980		Sheep	Earth	–	Yin
1980	16 Feb 1980 – 4 Feb 1981		Monkey	Metal	+	Yang
1981	5 Feb 1981 – 24 Jan 1982		Rooster	Metal	–	Yin
1982	25 Jan 1982 – 12 Feb 1983		Dog	Water	+	Yang
1983	13 Feb 1983 – 1 Feb 1984		Pig	Water	–	Yin
1984	2 Feb 1984 – 19 Feb 1985		Rat	Wood	+	Yang
1985	20 Feb 1985 – 8 Feb 1986		Ox	Wood	–	Yin
1986	9 Feb 1986 – 28 Jan 1987		Tiger	Fire	+	Yang
1987	29 Jan 1987 – 16 Feb 1988		Rabbit	Fire	–	Yin
1988	17 Feb 1988 – 5 Feb 1989		Dragon	Earth	+	Yang
1989	6 Feb 1989 – 26 Jan 1990		Snake	Earth	–	Yin
1990	27 Jan 1990 – 14 Feb 1991		Horse	Metal	+	Yang
1991	15 Feb 1991 – 3 Feb 1992		Sheep	Metal	–	Yin
1992	4 Feb 1992 – 22 Jan 1993		Monkey	Water	+	Yang
1993	23 Jan 1993 – 9 Feb 1994		Rooster	Water	–	Yin
1994	10 Feb 1994 – 30 Jan 1995		Dog	Wood	+	Yang
1995	31 Jan 1995 – 18 Feb 1996		Pig	Wood	–	Yin
1996	19 Feb 1996 – 7 Feb 1997		Rat	Fire	+	Yang
1997	8 Feb 1997 – 27 Jan 1998		Ox	Fire	–	Yin
1998	28 Jan 1998 – 15 Feb 1999		Tiger	Earth	+	Yang
1999	16 Feb 1999 – 4 Feb 2000		Rabbit	Earth	–	Yin
2000	5 Feb 2000 – 23 Jan 2001		Dragon	Metal	+	Yang
2001	24 Jan 2001 – 11 Feb 2002		Snake	Metal	–	Yin
2002	12 Feb 2002 – 31 Jan 2003		Horse	Water	+	Yang
2003	1 Feb 2003 – 21 Jan 2004		Sheep	Water	–	Yin
2004	22 Jan 2004 – 8 Feb 2005		Monkey	Wood	+	Yang
2005	9 Feb 2005 – 28 Jan 2006		Rooster	Wood	–	Yin
2006	29 Jan 2006 – 17 Feb 2007		Dog	Fire	+	Yang
2007	18 Feb 2007 – 6 Feb 2008		Pig	Fire	–	Yin

14

Introducing the Animals

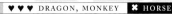

| THE RAT | ♥ ♥ ♥ DRAGON, MONKEY | ✖ HORSE |

Outwardly cool, Rats are passionate lovers with depths of feeling that others don't often recognize. Rats are very self-controlled.

| THE OX | ♥ ♥ ♥ SNAKE, ROOSTER | ✖ SHEEP |

Not necessarily the most romantic of the signs, Ox people make steadfast lovers as well as faithful, affectionate partners.

| THE TIGER | ♥ ♥ ♥ HORSE, DOG | ✖ MONKEY |

Passionate and sensual, Tigers are exciting lovers. Flirty when young, once committed they make stable partners and keep their sexual allure.

| THE RABBIT | ♥ ♥ ♥ SHEEP, PIG | ✖ ROOSTER |

Gentle, emotional and sentimental, Rabbits make sensitive lovers. They are shrewd and seek a partner who offers security.

| THE DRAGON | ♥ ♥ ♥ RAT, MONKEY | ✖ DOG |

Dragon folk get as much stimulation from mind-touch as they do through sex. A partner on the same wave-length is essential.

| THE SNAKE | ♥ ♥ ♥ OX, ROOSTER | ✖ PIG |

Deeply passionate, strongly sexed but not aggressive, snakes are attracted to elegant, refined partners. But they are deeply jealous and possessive.

♥ ♥ ♥ *COMPATIBLE* ✖ *INCOMPATIBLE*

THE HORSE   ♥ ♥ ♥ TIGER, DOG   ✖ RAT

For horse-born folk love is blind. In losing their hearts, they lose their heads and make several mistakes before finding the right partner.

15

THE SHEEP   ♥ ♥ ♥ RABBIT, PIG   ✖ OX

Sheep-born people are made for marriage. Domesticated home-lovers, they find emotional satisfaction with a partner who provides security.

THE MONKEY   ♥ ♥ ♥ DRAGON, RAT   ✖ TIGER

Clever and witty, Monkeys need partners who will keep them stimulated. Forget the 9 to 5 routine, these people need *pizzazz*.

THE ROOSTER   ♥ ♥ ♥ OX, SNAKE   ✖ RABBIT

The Rooster's stylish good looks guarantee they will attract many suitors. They are level-headed and approach relationships coolly.

THE DOG   ♥ ♥ ♥ TIGER, HORSE   ✖ DRAGON

A loving, stable relationship is an essential component in the lives of Dogs. Once they have found their mate, they remain faithful for life.

THE PIG   ♥ ♥ ♥ RABBIT, SHEEP   ✖ SNAKE

These are sensual hedonists who enjoy lingering love-making between satin sheets. Caviar and champagne go down very nicely too.

蛇

16

The Snake Personality

YEARS OF THE SNAKE

1905 ★ 1917 ★ 1929 ★ 1941 ★ 1953
1965 ★ 1977 ★ 1989 ★ 2001

ANCIENT WISDOM tells us that having a Snake in the household is a good omen since it means the family will never starve. Whether this is because Snake-born folk are shrewd in business, intuitive in their dealings or tenacious over their assets, one way or another they manage to attract money. It is unsurprising, therefore, that they are known as the guardians of the treasure. As a member of this tribe, you are unlikely to go without.

Only the best of everything, including food, will do for the sybaritic snake.

TREASURE

Treasure need not just refer to wealth; metaphorically, it may allude to your wisdom and depth of understanding. For you are the philosopher, the mystic of the astrological signs: perceptive, intuitive, even psychic some would say. That you're an attractive individual is indisputable. It isn't simply the fact that you're so chic, so cultured, so sophisticated and refined, but it's also that you're enigmatic. And who can resist a mystery?

蛇

Snakes know how to attract money and control cascading wealth.

A PRIVATE PERSON

Calm, reserved, quiet and contemplative, you're a private person who likes to play your cards very close to your chest. Often secretive and inscrutable, you're a subtle worker, adept at imperceptibly insinuating yourself and at handling people with Machiavellian precision and skill.

Der Kuß (detail)
EDVARD
MUNCH
1863–1944

SNAKE FACTS

Sixth in order ★ *Chinese name – She* ★ *Sign of Sagacity*
★ *Hour – 9AM – 10.59AM* ★ *Month – May* ★
★ *Western counterpart – Taurus* ★

CHARACTERISTICS

♥ *Subtlety* ♥ *Insight* ♥ *Shrewdness* ♥ *Discretion*
♥ *Wisdom* ♥ *Compassion*

✖ *Pride* ✖ *Indolence* ✖ *Manipulation* ✖ *Vanity*
✖ *Malice* ✖ *Possessiveness*

Your Hour of Birth

WHILE YOUR YEAR OF BIRTH describes your fundamental character, the Animal governing the actual hour in which you were born describes your outer temperament, how people see you or the picture you present to the outside world. Note that each Animal rules over two consecutive hours. Also note that these are GMT standard times and that adjustments need to be made if you were born during Summer or daylight saving time.

11PM – 12.59AM ★ RAT

 Pleasant, sociable, easy to get on with. An active, confident, busy person – and a bit of a busybody to boot.

1AM – 2.59AM ★ OX

 Level-headed and down-to-earth, you come across as knowledgeable and reliable – sometimes, though, a bit biased.

3AM – 4.59AM ★ TIGER

 Enthusiastic and self-assured, people see you as a strong and positive personality – at times a little over-exuberant.

5AM – 6.59AM ★ RABBIT

 You're sensitive and shy and don't project your real self to the world. You feel you have to put on an act to please others.

7AM – 8.59AM ★ DRAGON

 Independent and interesting, you present a picture of someone who is quite out of the ordinary.

9AM – 10.59AM ★ SNAKE

 You can be a bit difficult to fathom and, because you appear so controlled, people either take to you instantly, or not at all.

蛇

11AM – 12.59PM ★ HORSE

 Open, cheerful and happy-go-lucky is the picture you always put across to others. You're an extrovert and it generally shows.

1PM – 2.59PM ★ SHEEP

 Your unassuming nature won't allow you to foist yourself upon others so people see you as quiet and retiring – but eminently sensible, though.

3PM – 4.59PM ★ MONKEY

 Lively and talkative, that twinkle in your eye will guarantee you make friends wherever you go.

5PM – 6.59PM ★ ROOSTER

 There's something rather stylish in your approach that gives people an impression of elegance and glamour. But you don't suffer fools gladly.

7PM – 8.59PM ★ DOG

 Some people see you as steady and reliable, others as quiet and graceful and others still as dull and unimaginative. It all depends who you're with at the time.

9PM – 10.59PM ★ PIG

 Your laid-back manner conceals a depth of interest and intelligence that doesn't always come through at first glance.

Your hour of birth describes your outer temperament.

蛇

20

The Snake Lover

A lover of all pleasures of the flesh, you're a prime sensualist, happy to physically please your lover and to enjoy being pleasured in return. You like nothing better than lounging about and indulging your senses. You buy the best foods and wines, the most elegant clothes, the loveliest artworks for your home.

SLEEK AND SUAVE, SULTRY AND PASSIONATE, you're the original femme fatale or the dark, brooding hero about whom romantic novels are written by the truckload. Like all Snakes, you're physically beautiful and devastatingly sexy. Always stylish and well-groomed, you have that certain *je ne sais quoi* that people find so alluring but can't quite put their finger on. With your quiet charms you bewitch and intoxicate those around you. You exude immense gravitas and a feeling of intense emotional energy and pent-up sexual power – a truly seductive creature.

Sensual and sexy, snakes adore abandoning themselves to the swooning pleasures of love in the afternoon.

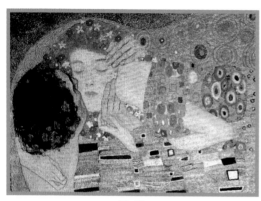

The Kiss
GUSTAV KLIMT 1862–1918

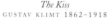

SELECTION

You are extremely discriminative and selective when it comes to the people you date and the choice of partner you make. In any relationship you're a decided asset not only because of your good looks, your charm and your refined tastes, but also because of your clever, incisive mind, your physical responsiveness and your odd-ball sense of humour.

SNAKE INTRIGUE

In love, you can become intense, jealous and possessive, yet you're not averse to the occasional extra-marital affair. Snakes absolutely adore gossip and intrigue; the thought of a secret love tryst is irresistible and fills you with frissons of excitement. However, if at any point in time you're crossed or betrayed, a ruthless and vituperative side to your nature will emerge and you go to any lengths to get even. Make no bones about it, Snake-born folk never forgive and never forget.

蛇

22

In Your Element

ALTHOUGH YOUR SIGN recurs every 12 years, each generation is slightly modified by one of 5 elements. If you were born under the Metal influence your character, emotions and behaviour would show significant variations from an individual born under one of the other elements. Check the Year Chart for your ruling element and discover what effects it has upon you.

THE METAL SNAKE ★ 1941 AND 2001

As a Metal Snake you have a gift for spotting openings and opportunities and you know how to get your feet under the table so fast that others don't even notice until it's too late. Money is important to you but so too is the desire for the *dolce vita*.

THE WATER SNAKE ★ 1953

With highly developed intuitive faculties and strong psychological insights, you can be powerfully psychic. Your forte lies in the management and organization of people and institutions. You go hell for leather in attaining your most cherished ambitions.

23

THE WOOD SNAKE ★ 1905 AND 1965

Probably the kindest, most amenable and altruistic of the elemental Snakes, you're not quite as narcissistic as the rest. You are genuinely concerned for others and prepared to share your knowledge for the good of mankind. You have exquisite tastes and excellent powers of discrimination.

THE FIRE SNAKE ★ 1917 AND 1977

Magnetic and charismatic, you've got what it takes to become an influential leader, and with your powers of persuasion, you have people hanging on your every word. The desire for money, power and fame drives you ever onwards and upwards.

THE EARTH SNAKE ★ 1929 AND 1989

With your logical, down-to-earth approach, you're not troubled with the characteristic paranoia that afflicts so many other Snakes. Consequently, you're more trusting and friendly, more considerate and honest. You succeed in the world of high finance by dint of your own sustained efforts.

24

*Rencontre
du Soir
(detail)*
THEOPHILE-
ALEXANDRE
STEINLEN
1859–1923

Partners in Love

THE CHINESE are very definite about which animals are compatible with each other and which are antagonistic. So find out if you're truly suited to your partner.

SNAKE + RAT ★ *If you both work on the differences in your characters, you could learn a great deal from each other.*

SNAKE + OX ★ *Sympathetic, understanding, loving, on the same wave-length – you've got the lot!*

SNAKE + TIGER ★ *Different outlook, different lifestyles and different objectives all suggests little meeting of minds.*

Eiaha ohipa
PAUL GAUGUIN
1848–1903

SNAKE + RABBIT ★ *Deep passions make this one heck of a sexy combo!*

SNAKE + DRAGON ★ *Clever and crafty, flirty and shirty – you fit together like two pieces of a jig-saw puzzle.*

SNAKE + SNAKE ★ *Intellectually, you make a great match. Emotionally, jealousy gets in the way.*

LOVE PARTNERS AT A GLANCE

Snake with:	Tips on Togetherness	Compatibility
Rat	an alluring fascination	♥♥♥
Ox	simply sublime	♥♥♥♥
Tiger	odds against	♥
Rabbit	great sex	♥♥♥
Dragon	mirror images	♥♥♥
Snake	maintain separate identities	♥♥
Horse	talking helps to sort it out	♥♥
Sheep	deeply satisfying	♥♥♥♥
Monkey	only with co-operation	♥♥
Rooster	solid!	♥♥♥♥
Dog	first comes the physical, then the mental	♥♥♥
Pig	deep divisions	♥

COMPATIBILITY RATINGS:
♥ *conflict* ♥♥ *work at it* ♥♥♥ *strong sexual attraction* ♥♥♥♥ *heavenly!*

蛇

25

SNAKE + HORSE ★
Different viewpoints, different
agendas spell poor prospects.

SNAKE + SHEEP ★
Terrific friends and sexy lovers.

SNAKE + MONKEY ★
You'll each be constantly looking
over your shoulder at the other.

SNAKE + ROOSTER ★
What a great team!

SNAKE + DOG ★
Mutual attraction on sight.

SNAKE + PIG ★
Alas, little common ground.

Snakes and
Horses may
not see eye to
eye in love
matters.

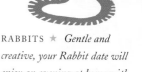

Hot Dates

IF YOU'RE DATING someone for the first time, taking your partner out for a special occasion or simply wanting to re-ignite that flame of passion between you, it helps to understand what would please that person most.

RATS ★ *Wine and dine him or take her to a party. Do something on impulse... go to the races or take a flight in a hot air balloon.*

OXEN ★ *Go for a drive in the country and drop in on a stately home. Visit an art gallery or antique shops. Then have an intimate dinner à deux.*

'So glad to see you...'
COCA-COLA 1945

TIGERS ★ *Tigers thrive on excitement so go clay-pigeon shooting, Formula One racing or challenge each other to a Quasar dual. A date at the theatre will put stars in your Tiger's eyes.*

RABBITS ★ *Gentle and creative, your Rabbit date will enjoy an evening at home with some take-away food and a romantic video. Play some seductive jazz and snuggle up.*

DRAGONS ★ *Mystery and magic will thrill your Dragon date. Take in a son et lumière show or go to a carnival. Or drive to the coast and sink your toes in the sand as the sun sets.*

SNAKES ★ *Don't do anything too active – these creatures like to take life sloooowly. Hire a row-boat for a long, lazy ride down the river. Give a soothing massage, then glide into a sensual jacuzzi together.*

蛇

The Carnival
GASTON-DOIN 19/20TH CENTURY

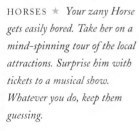

HORSES ★ *Your zany Horse gets easily bored. Take her on a mind-spinning tour of the local attractions. Surprise him with tickets to a musical show. Whatever you do, keep them guessing.*

SHEEP ★ *These folk adore the Arts so visit a museum, gallery or poetry recital. Go to a concert, the ballet, or the opera.*

MONKEYS ★ *The fantastical appeals to this partner, so go to a fancy-dress party or a masked ball, a laser light show or a sci-fi movie.*

ROOSTERS ★ *Grand gestures will impress your Rooster. Escort her to a film première or him to a formal engagement. Dressing up will place this date in seventh heaven.*

DOGS ★ *A cosy dinner will please this most unassuming of partners more than any social occasion. Chatting and story telling will ensure a close understanding.*

PIGS ★ *Arrange a slap-up meal or a lively party, or cruise through the shopping mall. Shopping is one of this partner's favourite hobbies!*

Detail from Chinese Marriage Ceremony
CHINESE PAINTING

Year of Commitment

CAN THE YEAR in which you marry (or make a firm commitment to live together) have any influence upon your marital relationship or the life you and your partner forge together? According to the Orientals, it certainly can. Whether your marriage is fiery, gentle, productive, passionate, insular or sociable doesn't so much depend on your animal nature, as on the nature of the Animal in whose year you tied the knot.

IF YOU MARRY IN A YEAR OF THE...

RAT ★ *your marriage should succeed because ventures starting now attract long-term success. Materially, you won't want and life is full of friendship.*

Marriage Feast
CHINESE PAINTING

OX ★ *your relationship will be solid and tastes conventional. Diligence will be recognized and you'll be well respected.*

TIGER ★ *you'll need plenty of humour to ride out the storms. Marrying in the Year of the Tiger is not auspicious.*

RABBIT ★ *you're wedded under the emblem of lovers. It's auspicious for a happy, carefree relationship, as neither partner wants to rock the boat.*

DRAGON ★ *you're blessed. This year is highly auspicious for luck, happiness and success.*

SNAKE ★ *it's good for romance but sexual entanglements are rife. Your relationship may seem languid, but passions run deep.*

HORSE ★ *chances are you decided to marry on the spur of the moment as the Horse year encourages impetuous behaviour. Marriage now may be volatile.*

SHEEP ★ *your family and home are blessed but watch domestic spending. Money is very easily frittered away.*

Marriage Ceremony
CHINESE PAINTING

MONKEY ★ *married life could be unconventional. As plans go awry your lives could be full of surprises.*

ROOSTER ★ *drama characterizes your married life. Your household will run like clockwork, but bickering could strain your relationship.*

DOG ★ *it's a truly fortunate year and you can expect domestic joy. Prepare for a large family as the Dog is the sign of fertility!*

PIG ★ *it's highly auspicious and there'll be plenty of fun. Watch out for indulgence and excess.*

Marriage Ceremony (detail)
CHINESE PAINTING

Detail from Chinese Marriage Ceremony
CHINESE PAINTING

蛇

30

TYPICAL SNAKE PLEASURES

COLOUR PREFERENCES ★ *Red*

Bloodstone

Topaz

Jasper

GEMS AND STONES ★ *Topaz, jasper, bloodstone*

SUITABLE GIFTS ★ *Solitaire, pack of Tarot cards, field glasses, religious icon, worry beads, snake-skin wallet, bath oil, diamond brooch, stamp collection, marble bust*

HOBBIES AND PASTIMES ★ *Fishing, numismatics, photography, visiting churches, diving, painting, scrying, astrology, orienteering*

HOLIDAY PREFERENCES ★ *Rest and relaxation are what you need on holiday. Check into a health farm and try all the treatments – the flotarium, thalassotherapy, reflexology and aromatherapy. Or get away from it all on a remote Aegean island or in a log cabin. Recharge your spiritual batteries on a retreat or contemplate life as you commune with Nature.*

Old fort, Delhi, India

COUNTRIES LINKED WITH THE SNAKE ★ *Russia, India, Mexico, Peru, Iran, Saudi Arabia*

The Snake Parent

31

*Snake
parents
protect their
little ones
from the
rigours of
the outside
world.*

THAT DROLL sense of humour of yours stands you in good stead when dealing with your offspring. Because you have the knack of seeing the odd or absurd side of things, you can often defuse a potentially explosive situation simply with a wry quip or a funny aside. Though you dearly love and instinctively protect your children, what you find difficult to handle are noisy, rumbustious scenes.

ROUGH AND TUMBLE

You're not one for rough and tumble and any hint of boisterousness has you running for the nearest sanctuary that will offer peace and quiet. Restoring order, laying down the law or dishing out the discipline, therefore, tends to fall on your partner's shoulders.

THE SNAKE HABITAT

In the Snake household, refinement prevails; in decorations and choice of furnishings, quality comes before quantity every time. Though red is the colour associated with your sign, if you use it in your décor, it will be applied subtly and muted shades confirm stylish elegance. Textures are chosen for their sensual feel, furniture for its deep comfort, artefacts for detail and effect, which altogether spell luxury. One house never seems to be enough for Snakes; they either move several times or have more than one home.

Animal Babies

FOR SOME parents, their children's personalities harmonize perfectly with their own. Others find that no matter how much they may love their offspring they're just not on the same wavelength. Our children arrive with their characters already well formed and, according to Chinese philosophy, shaped by the influence of their Animal Year. So you should be mindful of the year in which you conceive.

BABIES BORN IN THE YEAR OF THE...

RAT ★ *love being cuddled. They keep on the go – so give them plenty of rest. Later they enjoy collecting things.*

OX ★ *are placid, solid and independent. If not left to their own devices they sulk.*

TIGER ★ *are happy and endearing. As children, they have irrepressible energy. Boys are sporty and girls tom-boys.*

RABBIT ★ *are sensitive and strongly bonded to their mother. They need stability to thrive.*

DRAGON ★ *are independent and imaginative from the start. Encourage any interest that will allow their talents to flourish.*

SNAKE ★ *have great charm. They are slow starters so may need help with school work. Teach them to express feelings.*

蛇

33

One Hundred Children Scroll
ANON, MING PERIOD

HORSE ★ *will burble away contentedly for hours. Talking starts early and they excel in languages.*

SHEEP ★ *are placid, well-behaved and respectful. They are family-oriented and never stray too far from home.*

MONKEY ★ *take an insatiable interest in everything. With agile minds they're quick to learn. They're good-humoured but mischievous!*

ROOSTER ★ *are sociable. Bright and vivacious, their strong adventurous streak best shows itself on a sports field.*

DOG ★ *are cute and cuddly. Easily pleased, they are content just pottering around the house amusing themselves for hours. Common sense is their greatest virtue.*

PIG ★ *are affectionate and friendly. Well-balanced, self-confident children, they're happy-go-lucky and laid-back. They are popular with friends.*

*The white-
hot heat of
technology
is not
for the
languorous
snake.*

Health, Wealth and Worldly Affairs

IT'S BEST if you steer clear of noisy, chaotic situations since these upset you and frazzle your nerves. Some people may enjoy the adrenaline surge that goes with physical challenge and conflict, but *not* you. You need calm at all times. If you want to stay healthy, don't burn the candle at both ends. Plenty of rest and sleep is the Snake's formula for a long life.

CAREER

Snake-born people go through several major transitions in their working lives, often changing career at least twice so you're unlikely to be attracted by mundane jobs. Whatever you do, you bring

Practical yet intuitive, you play your cards close to your chest and work far better alone than in a group. Never impulsive, you prefer to gather and assimilate information before making judgements, but you do score by following your hunches.

concentration, an eye for detail and laser-like precision to your job. You're blessed with organizational skills and the ability to put your finger right on the problem.

FINANCES

Financially, as long as you follow your instincts you'll be successful. However, you must avoid impulse-buying or making rash judgements because, although you are intuitive, you are also a poor gambler. Wild speculation for a Snake can bring disaster.

Snakes love an elegant, intimate soirée with a well-chosen friend and a spicy side-dish of juicy gossip.

蛇

35

FRIENDSHIPS

Though you're generally a quiet and solitary creature, you're not averse to social get-togethers — especially grand functions or elegant dinner parties. You don't enjoy small talk yet you like nothing better than a good gossip spiced up with a bit of juicy scandal. As you're highly selective about whom you allow to come close to you, you don't make friends easily but those you do make stay friends for life.

Yours is a lucky sign and, since you're shrewd, you're unlikely ever to be seriously penniless. You have expensive tastes and spend extravagantly, yet it's odds on that you'll end up very comfortably off.

SNAKES MAKE EXCELLENT:

★ Scientists ★ Technologists ★ Researchers ★ Analysts ★
★ Potters ★ Painters ★ Musicians ★ Jewellers ★ Mystics ★
★ Silversmiths ★ Spiritual leaders ★ Investigators ★
★ Politicians ★ Psychologists ★ Surgeons ★ Sociologists ★
★ Philosophers ★ Astrologers ★ Magicians ★ Dieticians ★

蛇

East Meets West

COMBINE YOUR Oriental Animal sign with your Western Zodiac birth sign to form a deeper and richer understanding of your character and personality.

ARIES SNAKE

★ *You have a good deal more get-up-and-go than most* Snakes. At work your shrewd intelligence guarantees success. You're passionate and never afraid to take the initiative.

TAUREAN SNAKE

★ *Although not the most energetic person in the world, you* possess one of the keenest minds around. Love, security, comfort and wealth are essential to you.

GEMINI SNAKE

★ *You're chatty, witty and sexy! If flirting were an* Olympic sport, you'd run away with the gold! You're not the most faithful of partners but when you're around, life is always fun.

CANCERIAN SNAKE

★ *A twinkling star, you're attracted to the limelight. You* work to feather your nest and decorate your house tastefully. Family and home are the centre of your universe.

LEONINE SNAKE

★ *You need enough encouragement to function well, but* not so much that it swells your head, so a lover who gets the balance right is essential.

VIRGO SNAKE

★ *Ambitious and bossy, you like to be in charge. Intellectual* rather than emotional, you're not demonstrative in love, but are a dedicated home-maker, and use all your energy to improve your status.

蛇

37

LIBRAN SNAKE

★ You're recherché, cultured and full of savoir faire. With your social graces and persuasive charm, is it any wonder that suitors gather around you like bees drawn to honey? One of life's romantics, you're in love with love.

SCORPIO SNAKE

★ Slinky and street-wise, your pheromones are so strong they can be picked up way over the other side of town. An enigma to all those who know you, you are a deep, passionate and jealous person who never forgives and never forgets.

SAGITTARIAN SNAKE

★ Your sagacity and integrity go before you. Far-sighted and intuitive, you succeed by following your instincts and good taste in your occupation and your private life. Elegant and classy, or suave and debonair, you seek a partner to share a deep and spiritual relationship.

CAPRICORN SNAKE

★ It's with careful, planning that you build your reputation, position and wealth. At home or at work you go for the best in everything. A bit of a snob, your heart's in the right place and your feet firmly on the ground.

AQUARIAN SNAKE

★ Intellectual but idealistic, possessive but broad-minded, you're full of contradictions. You need the love of a mate, but you are frightened at the thought of being tied down. You get as much gratification from a good chat as from a session between the sheets.

PISCEAN SNAKE

★ You are probably the most sensitive of the Snakes, sensual, dreamy and easily wounded, taking the merest slight to heart. You're ruled by your emotions, especially by the heart, and when you fall in love, you go hook, line and sinker, and you commit yourself for life.

FAMOUS SNAKES

Queen Elizabeth I   Muhammad Ali

Audrey Hepburn   J.F.Kennedy   Dostoievski

Mahatma Gandhi   Mao Tse-Tung   Jacqueline Kennedy Onassis

Bob Dylan ★ Kim Basinger ★ André Previn
Delia Smith ★ Oprah Winfrey
Stefan Edberg ★ Nigel Mansell ★ Ryan O'Neal
Paul Hogan ★ Dionne Warwick
Muhammad Ali ★ Ruby Wax ★ Vera Lynn
John F Kennedy ★ Dostoievski ★ Picasso
Jacqueline Kennedy Onassis ★ Audrey Hepburn
Queen Elizabeth I ★ Mao Tse-Tung
Abraham Lincoln ★ Mahatma Gandhi

Pablo Picasso

The Snake Year in Focus

AFTER THE DRAMAS of the Year of the Dragon, Snake Years come as watershed periods, restoring order and bringing in comparative peace. This year, we can all quietly draw breath and slowly reassess our situation.

DUPLICITY

It would be wise not to take anything on trust. There's a decided duplicity in the air and it is advisable to read the small print carefully. Because snakes are associated with treachery, political machinations and conspiracy will be rife; international affairs are likely to be peppered with shady dealings.

FERTILITY SYMBOL

As the snake is a symbol of fertility, issues concerning conception and morality will be aired and headlines will reveal sex scandals in high places. This year heralds an economic upturn and markets will be buoyant, especially in Arts and communications. The fashion-conscious will favour sophistication.

ACTIVITIES ASSOCIATED WITH THE SNAKE YEAR

The discovery, invention, patenting, marketing or manufacturing of: IQ tests, rings of Uranus, the Oscar awards, Chanel fashions, DNA, spread of psychology.

40

Your Snake Fortunes
for the Next 12 Years

1996 MARKS THE BEGINNING of a new 12-year cycle in the Chinese calendar. How your relationships and worldly prospects fare will depend on the influence of each Animal year in turn.

1996 YEAR OF THE RAT   `19 Feb 1996 – 6 Feb 1997`

Though not a fast-paced creature, you'll find the lively scenario presented by this year invigorating as it inspires you to spark off new ideas. If you want to pursue different avenues, this is a good time to seize the opportunities that 1996 has in store.

YEAR TREND: A BUSY YEAR

1997 YEAR OF THE OX   `7 Feb 1997 – 27 Jan 1998`

1997 will be an auspicious year for you with a steady pace highly conducive to your nature. You'll get results by allowing your intuitive faculties free rein and by acting on your hunches.

YEAR TREND: STRIKE WHILE THE IRON IS HOT

1998 YEAR OF THE TIGER `28 Jan 1998 – 15 Feb 1999`

Tiger Years are often fraught with furious activity and hidden dangers, which is quite inimical to you. So 1998 will not be an easy time for you and you should stay on the sidelines until the stampede is over. Emotions, too, are volatile.

YEAR TREND: KEEP A LOW PROFILE

1999 YEAR OF THE RABBIT | *16 Feb 1999 – 4 Feb 2000*

Socializing and attending cultural events will take up a lot of your time, especially if you're connected with the beauty business. Beware entanglements or sexual intrigue as indiscretion could cost you dear.

YEAR TREND: A TIME FOR PRUDENCE AND CIRCUMSPECTION

2000 YEAR OF THE DRAGON | *5 Feb 2000 – 23 Jan 2001*

Last year's rumours rumble on and add fuel to the roller-coaster events of this dramatic year. As someone who thrives on tranquillity, you will find the atmosphere unsettling but, take heart, conserve strength and money and wait for the hubbub to blow over.

YEAR TREND: WATCH AND WAIT

Snakes can celebrate success in the year of the Snake.

2001 YEAR OF THE SNAKE | *24 Jan 2001 – 11 Feb 2002*

Hurrah! This is *your* year. It's a time when you can make major advances and your efforts come to fruition. Ambitions can be realized now and talents rewarded. Acknowledge those who love and support you as you rise up the ladder and improve your standing.

YEAR TREND: PERSONALLY SATISFYING

42

2002 YEAR OF THE HORSE *12 Feb 2002 – 31 Jan 2003*

This year, occupational matters are likely to fare much better than affairs of the heart. At work you can make good progress but beware of those Machiavellian tactics that you are so fond of.

YEAR TREND: KEEP ALL YOUR DEALINGS ABOVE BOARD

2003 YEAR OF THE SHEEP *1 Feb 2003 – 21 Jan 2004*

Sticking to the tried and tested this year will yield results. Put major new plans aside for another year when they will enjoy a more favourable reception. Maintain a high profile because contacts you make now will prove, both personally and professionally, beneficial.

YEAR TREND: GLAMOUR BRINGS SUCCESS

2004 YEAR OF THE MONKEY *22 Jan 2004 – 8 Feb 2005*

Appearances can be deceptive in the Year of the Monkey, so check your facts and don't underestimate colleagues, lovers or opponents. Taking sides will only compromise your integrity; but love ties strengthen and intimate relationships bring joy.

YEAR TREND: A TIME FOR SITTING ON THE FENCE

Seize the opportunities as they occur.

蛇

2005 YEAR OF THE ROOSTER | *9 Feb 2005 – 28 Jan 2006*

Don't let early set-backs demoralize you; your prospects will improve as the year progresses. At work, your efforts will be rewarded. At home, harmony reigns and time spent with partners and loved ones will compensate for any worldly upsets.

YEAR TREND: FINANCIALLY EXPENSIVE BUT EMOTIONALLY SATISFYING

2006 YEAR OF THE DOG | *29 Jan 2006 – 17 Feb 2007*

Prepare for a year full of activity. Putting into motion ideas that have been on the back burner will bring results, and fresh initiatives will snowball and attract financial rewards seemingly with little effort.

YEAR TREND: BEING SECURITY-MINDED PAYS OFF

2007 YEAR OF THE PIG | *18 Feb 2007 – 6 Feb 2008*

For you, 2007 could be a difficult year in which for every three steps you take forwards, you're compelled to take two back. However, any impulsive action to recoup lost ground will only backfire. The best advice is simply to bide your time.

YEAR TREND: FRUSTRATING

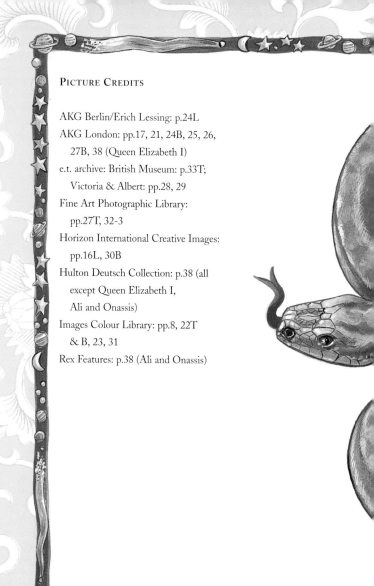

PICTURE CREDITS

AKG Berlin/Erich Lessing: p.24L
AKG London: pp.17, 21, 24B, 25, 26,
    27B, 38 (Queen Elizabeth I)
e.t. archive: British Museum: p.33T;
    Victoria & Albert: pp.28, 29
Fine Art Photographic Library:
    pp.27T, 32-3
Horizon International Creative Images:
    pp.16L, 30B
Hulton Deutsch Collection: p.38 (all
    except Queen Elizabeth I,
    Ali and Onassis)
Images Colour Library: pp.8, 22T
    & B, 23, 31
Rex Features: p.38 (Ali and Onassis)